Christm Treasures

GW00482931

1

Christmas Treasures

The first record for the celebration of Jesus Christ's birth on the 25th December is found in a Roman document dated AD 336.

The date was chosen as a Christian replacement of the Roman festival celebrating the unconquerable sun.

So instead of worshipping the sun, Christians began to use the festival to celebrate the birthday of Jesus Christ and to worship instead the unconquerable Son.

The word *'Christmas'* comes from Old English *'Cristes Masse'*, which means *'Festival Mass of Christ'*.

A White Christmas

The definition of a white Christmas is when one snowflake falls on the roof of the London Weather Centre.

There were only seven white Christmases in England throughout the twentieth century. So far in the twenty-first century, the Meteorological Office in London has recorded snow falling on Christmas Day in 2004, 2009 and 2010.

Twelve days

Have you ever heard the hidden meaning behind the 'Twelve Days of Christmas'? What in the world do leaping lords, French hens, swimming swans and especially the partridge who won't come out of the pear tree, have to do with Christmas?

In case you've always wondered why we have this seemingly crazy Christmas song, here's one answer:

From 1558 until 1829, Roman Catholics in England were not permitted to practise their faith openly. So, someone wrote this carol as a teaching song for young Catholics. It had two levels of meaning: the surface meaning plus a hidden meaning known only to members of their church. Each element in the carol has a code word for a religious reality, which the children could remember.

The partridge in a pear tree was Jesus Christ.

Two turtledoves were the Old and New Testaments.

Three French hens stood for faith, hope and love.

The four calling birds were the four gospels of Matthew, Mark, Luke and John.

The five golden rings recalled the Torah or Law, the first five books of the Old Testament.

The six geese a-laying stood for the six days of creation.

Seven swans a-swimming represented the seven gifts of the Holy Spirit: *Prophecy, Serving, Teaching, Exhortation, Contribution, Leadership* and *Mercy*.

The eight maids a-milking were the eight beatitudes.

Nine ladies dancing were the nine fruits of the Holy Spirit: *Love, Joy, Peace, Patience, Kindness, Goodness, Faithfulness, Gentleness* and *Self Control*.

The ten lords a-leaping were the Ten Commandments.

The eleven pipers piping stood for the eleven faithful disciples.

The twelve drummers drumming symbolized the twelve points of belief in The Apostles' Creed.

cards

Cards are sent as an expression of goodwill at Christmas time.

The first Christmas card was commissioned in 1843 by Sir Henry Cole, the founder of the Victoria & Albert Museum in London. In November 1843 he wrote in his diary, *'Mr John Horsley came and brought me a design for a Christmas card.'* It showed a family celebrating Christmas. On each side of the main panel, a picture showed charitable acts; one, *'Clothing the Naked'* and the other *'Feeding the Hungry'*. The cards were all hand-coloured! The first Christmas card's inscription read: *'Merry Christmas and a happy New Year to you.'*

It took another twenty years for the idea to really catch on, bu when it did – it did! The Royal Ma reports that in the UK we send 1. billion Christmas cards each year

Crackers

Christmas crackers were invented by Tom Smith in 1840. He was a confectioner and while on holiday in Paris he came across sugared almonds wrapped in coloured paper. In those days British sweets were sold unwrapped and the French style appealed to him. Smith also heard about the Chinese tradition of putting mottos in with sweets, so, when he returned to London, he tried the idea adding mottos, proverbs and riddles. Sales were low until, one day, when Tom was gazing into a fire watching the logs crackling, he had the idea of putting in a little bang. He started adding toys, jokes, jewellery, perfume and other surprises.

Crackers have remained popular for over a century and show no sign of losing their Christmas appeal.

Carols

The earliest Christmas carols date back to the fifth century in France. The first carol was titled 'Jesus, Light of All Nations'. It was written by St Hilary of Poitiers. The word 'carole' means to dance and play the flute.

Crib

Having a model version of the nativity came from Francis of Assisi in the thirteenth century. Francis wanted to make a visual aid to illustrate the reality of the birth of Christ, in all its poverty and discomfort.

He found a cave on a mountainside near the village of Greccio. He brought a donkey and an ox and had the figure of a baby carved and laid in a manger. News of what he was doing spread all over the countryside and many people came to visit.

9

The Birth of Jesus Foretold

**The Bible
Luke 1:26–38**

In the sixth month of Elizabeth's pregnancy, God sent the angel Gabriel to Nazareth, a village in Galilee, to a virgin named Mary. She was engaged to be married to a man named Joseph, a descendant of King David. Gabriel appeared to her and said, *'Greetings, favoured woman! The Lord is with you!'*

Confused and disturbed, Mary tried to think what the angel could mean. *'Don't be frightened, Mary,'* the angel told her, *'for God has decided to bless you! You will become pregnant and have a son, and you are to name him Jesus. He will be very great and will be called the Son of the Most High. And the Lord God will give him the throne of his ancestor David. And he will reign over Israel forever, his Kingdom will never end!'*

Mary asked the angel, *'But how can I have a baby? I am a virgin.'* The angel replied, *'The Holy Spirit will come upon you, and the power of the Most High will overshadow you. So the baby born to you will be holy, and he will be called the Son of God. What's more, your relative Elizabeth has become pregnant in her old age! People used to say she was barren, but she's already in her sixth month. For nothing is impossible with God.'*

Mary responded, *'I am the Lord's servant, and I am willing to accept whatever he wants. May everything you have said come true.'* And then the angel left.

Holly

Evergreen plants originally reminded people that some forms of life continued through the winter, when most of nature appeared to have gone to sleep.

The holly's white flower has been interpreted as the purity of Mary the mother of Jesus; its prickly leaves as the crown of thorns placed on Jesus' head when he was crucified by the Romans; and its red berries signify the drops of blood he shed on the cross and the promise of new life to come when he rose from the dead.

Today it is customary to hang a holly wreath on the front door.

Nine Lessons

The popular Nine Lessons and Carols service was designed by Archbishop Edward Benson in 1883 and adapted for use in King's College Chapel, Cambridge by Eric Milner-White when he was Dean in 1918. It became world famous when the BBC began to broadcast the service which has happened each year since regular broadcasting began in the late 1920s.

When we celebrate birthdays we don't usually retell the story of the person's birth at children's parties. We don't tell relatives and friends about the pregnancy, or about the feelings of Mum and Dad when they heard they were going to have a baby. Yet every Christmas we sing carols and read lessons about 'baby-talk' details.

The Birth of Jesus

Luke 2:1–7

'At that time the Roman emperor, Augustus, decreed that a census should be taken throughout the Roman Empire. (This was the first census taken when Quirinius was governor of Syria.) All returned to their own towns to register for this census. And because Joseph was a descendant of King David, he had to go to Bethlehem in Judea, David's ancient home. He travelled there from the village of Nazareth in Galilee. He took with him Mary, his fiancée, who was obviously pregnant by this time.

And while they were there, the time came for her baby to be born. She gave birth to her first child, a son. She wrapped him snugly in strips of cloth and laid him in a manger, because there was no room for them in the village inn.'

Incarnation

Incarnation is a Latin word that means, *'taking flesh'*. God *'took flesh'* and became the human Jesus.

He who was great became small.

He who was powerful became weak.

He who was rich became poor.

Surprise and amazement. How incomprehensible it is for a battleship to fit into a bath-tub or a skyscraper into a doll's house. Yet the God of infinity became a baby. But a baby can't rescue anyone. Babies constantly need rescuing themselves.

The Christ-child in complete humility is the key to life. In all history there is nothing like this. Stroll through the capitals of great nations into the public squares of large cities and you will undoubtedly come upon imposing monuments to outstanding men and women. But did you ever in your life see the statue of a famous man or woman as an infant? We don't look up at Nelson's Column in Trafalgar Square and see Nelson in a pushchair! Jesus Christ was honoured the day he was born. There was a big difference between the Garden of Eden and the cave at Bethlehem. In Eden, humankind was made in the image and likeness of God. But in Bethlehem, God was made in the image and likeness of humankind.

Santa Claus

Santa Claus began life as a fourth-century bishop called Nicholas in Myra, in what is now south-west Turkey.

A story is told of a very poor and desperate widower with three daughters who all needed dowries to get married. Hearing of their need, Nicholas dropped a bag of gold into the chimney, which fell into a stocking hung up to dry.

Nicholas is particularly popular in Holland, where he is called Sinter Klaas. It is there that the customs linking Nicholas to Christmas seem to have first begun.

It was the American poet Clement Clarke Moore who popularized Santa Claus after he wrote the poem 'A Visit from St Nicholas' in 1822, which begins, 'Twas the night before Christmas . . . '

And it was Thoma Nast who became Santa's first 'tailor In *Harper's Illustrated Weekly* in 1863 he drew Santa on a sleigh with a beard and full coat.

The rest is history!

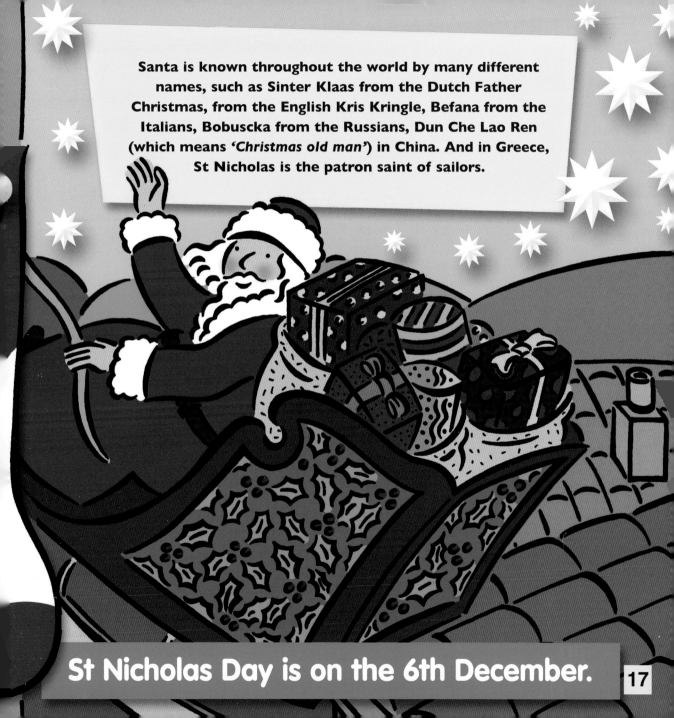

Santa is known throughout the world by many different names, such as Sinter Klaas from the Dutch Father Christmas, from the English Kris Kringle, Befana from the Italians, Bobuscka from the Russians, Dun Che Lao Ren (which means *'Christmas old man'*) in China. And in Greece, St Nicholas is the patron saint of sailors.

St Nicholas Day is on the 6th December.

17

Trees

Five million trees are grown to meet the demand for Christmas trees. Even with sophisticated fibre optic ones, people still prefer a real tree!

Norway sends a Christmas tree for London's Trafalgar Square as a gift every year as a thank you to the British people for their help during World War II. The first tree arrived in 1947.

The Christmas tree story originates in the eighth century with a man called Winfrith from Crediton in Devon, England. Winfrith later became known as Boniface and went to Germany to teach the Christian faith. One December Boniface found a group of people standing beneath an oak tree. They were preparing to sacrifice a child, believing that it would bring them good fortune. Boniface rescued the child and had the oak tree chopped down. As the oak tree fell, a small fir tree appeared in its place. Boniface suggested the fir tree was an emblem of the new faith he had brought to Germany. The tree's evergreen leaves were a symbol of life and he gave the fir tree the name 'Tree of the Christ-child'.

Years later a man called Martin Luther was walking one Christmas Eve under a clear night sky lit by hundreds of stars. The sight so moved him that he returned home with a fir tree and fixed candles to its branches to represent Jesus, the light of the world.

It was not until 1841 that the Christmas tree was introduced into Britain by Queen Victoria's husband, Prince Albert. From then on the tree became a central feature of the family Christmas. The star was added as a reminder of the star, which led the Magi to Jesus.

Turkey

Ninety-three per cent of the population in the UK will eat turkey on Christmas Day; this means eleven million turkeys being cooked!

Most people only eat turkey at Christmas – an old Christmas custom of eating something different on Christmas Day.

The turkey was brought to Europe in 1525 by Sebastian Cabot on a return journey from North America, which is where the birds came from. They were named turkeys in England because merchants from Turkey marketed them.

In 1851, the turkey received royal approval when it replaced the swan as the Christmas bird of Queen Victoria and her family.

Mince Pies

Mince pies were originally made of shredded meat in an oval cradle-shaped case to represent the manger in which Jesus was laid, and included three spices as a reminder of the three gifts from the Wise Men. It used to be customary to eat a mince pie on each of the twelve days of Christmas to ensure a happy year!

This delicacy outraged the puritans, so, in 1650 Oliver Cromwell passed an Act of Parliament authorizing the imprisonment of anyone found guilty of eating a mince pie. They were considered to be indulgent and far too rich.

In 1660 the mince pie returned and became more and more popular.

In the 19th century, a new sweeter mince pie arrived and instead of offering it at the beginning of the meal, it was offered at the end.

Magi

The **'Magi from the East'** whose journey from distant lands to see Jesus may have been the fulfilment of the words of the Old Testament prophet Isaiah: **'Nations will come to your light and kings to the brightness of your dawn'.**

The 6th January, the last day of
'The Twelve Days of Christmas' which
began on Christmas Day, is called
Epiphany, which means, 'appearing'.
It is the occasion when Jesus
revealed himself to these visitors.

For these Wise Men from the East,
Bethlehem was the journey's end.
The beginning had unfolded
hundreds of miles back, when a star
flared in the sky. Earnest
people and seekers of the
truth, they followed
the star until they
arrived at the
house where the
Christ-child was.
The event
was a miracle from God.

'They entered the house where the
child and his mother, Mary, were, and
they fell down before him and
worshipped him. Then they opened
their treasure chests and gave him gifts
of gold, frankincense, and myrrh.'

Matthew 2:11

The Wise Men remind us that
wisdom is not an accumulation of
facts, but an appreciation of
important truths.

23

Angels

This child was not only new, he was news. And angels proclaimed it in the skies. It was the front page of the gospel – and the word 'gospel' means 'good news'.

The word angel means 'messenger'. Angels act as God's agents. The Angel Gabriel appeared to Zachariah, who was a priest in the temple, giving him the news of a son, who would become John the Baptist, who prophesied Jesus' coming. Gabriel also declared to Mary that she would be the mother of Jesus. An angel appeared to Joseph and warned him to take Jesus and Mary and flee to Egypt. King Herod was planning to kill all the boys under the age of two so that Jesus, whom the Wise Men had called a king, would be killed.

Orville and Wilbur Wright had tried repeatedly to fly a heavier-than-air craft. Finally, on December 17th 1903, it happened. They managed to fly their plane about 120 feet! They actually flew! Elated, they had done what had never been done by anyone before, they wired a telegram with this news back home to their sister Katherine: *'We have actually flown 120 feet. Will be home for Christmas.'*

She ran down the street all excited, and showed the telegram, which was the news scoop of the century, to the city editor of the local daily paper in Dayton, Ohio. The next day he had headlined the story like this: *'LOCAL BICYCLE MERCHANTS TO BE HOME FOR CHRISTMAS!'*

Talk about missing it! This Christmas, don't miss the real story.

The Christmas pantomime is a unique British creation. It's from the pantomimes that we have catchphrases like, *'He's behind you!'* and *'Oh no he's not – Oh yes he is!'* It is at a pantomime that we experience the fun of booing and hissing.

The roots of our modern pantomimes go back to the old Christmas plays that were presented by street performers called *'Mummers'*.

The first pantomime was staged by the actor John Rich on the 26th December 1717 in London, at the Lincoln's Inn Fields Theatre. It was called *'Harlequin Executed'*. One of its key features was a number of dramatic transformations in which, with a wave of a wand, one scene changed into another.

As the years passed, others added their traditions until the fairy tale became a noisy spectacular.

The abbreviation *'Xmas'* has been in use for over 600 years. The X represents the Greek letter *'Chi'* which is the first letter of *'Christos'*, meaning Christ. So Xmas is not slang!

The poinsettia is a beautiful plant which is known as *'The Flower of the Holy Night'*.

In 1825, the United States appointed Joel Poinsett to become their first minister to Mexico. Poinsett was also an amateur botanist and he became fascinated by this unusual red-leaved shrub, whose leaves change colour when exposed to sunlight. When he returned to the United States in 1829, he took the plant with him. Because the plant bloomed in midwinter, it soon became one of the most popular Christmas plants and was named after its discoverer.

As well as being displayed as a living indoor plant at Christmas time, it has become a common motif on many Christmas decorations.

The person responsible for starting the broadcast was Lord Reith, who was the General Manager of the British Broadcasting Company when it started in 1922.

Lord Reith felt that the power of this new medium, the wireless, should be used to create a moment of national unity, with the King speaking to the nation as if to a single family. However, King George V declined this opportunity.

In 1927, the British Broadcasting Company became the British Broadcasting Corporation, and Lord Reith became its first Director General. In 1932 the BBC had begun its overseas Empire Service, so Lord Reith asked the King again – giving him the opportunity to speak to his subjects all over the world.

So, at 3pm on the 25th December 1932 from Sandringham, King George V made his first Christmas broadcast. It was the first time that many people had heard the King's voice delivering a personal message.

Why the Queen Christmas Day?

The King's speech was written for him by the author Rudyard Kipling and the wording made a significant impression and impact. *'I speak now, from my home and heart to you all.'* The King continued to make his Christmas broadcast each year until he died in 1936. The tradition would then have passed on to his son Edward, but before Christmas Day 1936, he abdicated the throne.

The new king, George VI, took over until he died in 1952 when his daughter Queen Elizabeth continued.

In 1957, the Christmas speech was televised for the first time and the royal broadcast has remained anchored at 3pm on Christmas Day.

Christmas

At that time the Emperor Augustus ordered a census to be taken throughout the Roman Empire. A man called Joseph went from the town of Bethlehem in Galilee, to the town of David in Judea. He went to register with Mary who was promised in marriage to him. While they were there, the time came for her to have her baby.

She gave birth to her first-born son, wrapped him in strips of cloth and laid him in a manger; there was no room for them to stay in the inn.

There were some shepherds in that part of the country who were spending the night in the fields, taking care of their flocks.

An angel of the Lord appeared to them, and the glory of the Lord shone over them. They were terribly afraid, but the angel said to them, *'Don't be afraid! I am here with good news for you, which will bring great joy to all the people.*

This very day in the city of David your Saviour was born – Christ the Lord. You will find the baby wrapped in strips of cloth and lying in a manger.'

Suddenly, a great army of heaven's angels appeared, singing praises to God, *'Glory to God in the highest heaven, and peace on earth to those with whom he is pleased.'*

When the angels went away from them back into heaven, the shepherds said to one another, *'Let's go to Bethlehem and see this thing that has happened which the Lord has told us.'* So they hurried off and found Mary and Joseph and saw the baby lying in the manger.

word search

Can you find the words highlighted on the left in our wordsearch?
Words can read in any direction, up, down or across.

```
X S J S F L M Y W C V R O O M I R
V Z H Z E O X A M V R C D O O G R
D E D T B R T C N R T H G M T B E
T P O J E D K I H G G J O S E P H
S D G F P R L E O R E A Q J G S E
I I Q X L M A G M Z O R D L A C B
R V S N E O E Z S P E M Z I L K X
H A K D H H C H A W I K A T I H K
C D S G R T N K E N E R G N L J C
O I I V Y E P U S L E B E G E C M
V Y M I R R H P Q C H R R Z E L Y
W Y V R A W J P A V C T Y O R I B
T G A I M B W E E A R S E R Z K A
L I S D Y E P G M H N J V B O E B
L E P G D I N G W J S G K N X L Z
S X Z A K G N I G N I S E F Y D G
Q B O K S A V I O U R P M L Z V I
```

Mary

Jesus did what no human being could ever do – he chose his own mother – and he chose Mary. For nine months, her body became more precious than anything on earth, and for the years that followed, she mothered the Son of God. Mary did everything a devoted mother could do for her son whom she knew was no ordinary man.

No woman has been as highly honoured and esteemed as has Mary by millions of people in all the world through the centuries. Madonnas abound in which skilled artists and sculptors have tried to imagine what she looked like. What she did have was beauty of character.

When the Angel Gabriel announced to Mary that she was to have a son to be called Jesus, he greeted her with the words *'The Lord is with you'*. What is so amazing is the way Mary received the news. She was in no way sceptical and doubtful. She asked intelligent, searching questions of Gabriel as to how she could become pregnant as she was a virgin. When Gabriel explained how she would be filled with God's spirit, Mary, with a tremendous act of faith, replied, *'May it be to me as you have said.'*

God did not go to a city, but to a remote and obscure village – not to a palace, but a poor house – not to the great and learned, but to the ordinary. The gentle and humble Mary was God's choice as the mother of Jesus.